Published in 2015 by The Rosen Publishing Group, Inc.
29 East 21st Street, New York, NY 10010

Photo Credits: **KEY** t=top; l=left; r=right; tl=top left; tcl=top center left; tc=top center; tcr=top center right; tr=top right; cl=center left; c=center; cr=center right; b=bottom; bl=bottom left; bcl=bottom center left; bc=bottom center; bcr=bottom center right; br=bottom right; bg=background

iS = istockphoto.com; PDCD = PhotoDisc; SH = Shutterstock; TPL = photolibrary.com

6cl iS; **15**tr PDCD; **18**tr iS; **26**tr SH; **30**bg CBCD; c iS; tc, tr, cr, br SH; bc TPL; **31**bg CBCD

All illustrations copyright Weldon Owen Pty Ltd

WELDON OWEN PTY LTD
Managing Director: Kay Scarlett
Creative Director: Sue Burk
Publisher: Helen Bateman
Senior Vice President, International Sales: Stuart Laurence
Vice President Sales North America: Ellen Towell
Administration Manager, International Sales: Kristine Ravn

Library of Congress Cataloging-in-Publication Data

Costain, Meredith, author.
 Mammals great and small / by Meredith Costain.
     pages cm — (Discovery education. Animals)
 Includes index.
 ISBN 978-1-4777-6940-9 (library binding) — ISBN 978-1-4777-6941-6 (pbk.) —
ISBN 978-1-4777-6942-3 (6-pack)
 1. Mammals—Juvenile literature. 2. Mammals—Evolution—Juvenile literature. I. Title.
 QL706.2.C67 2015
 599—dc23
                              2013047539

Manufactured in the United States of America

CPSIA Compliance Information: Batch #WS14PK3: For Further Information contact Rosen Publishing, New York, New York at 1-800-237-9932

ANIMALS

MAMMALS
GREAT AND SMALL

Meredith Costain

PowerKiDS
press

New York

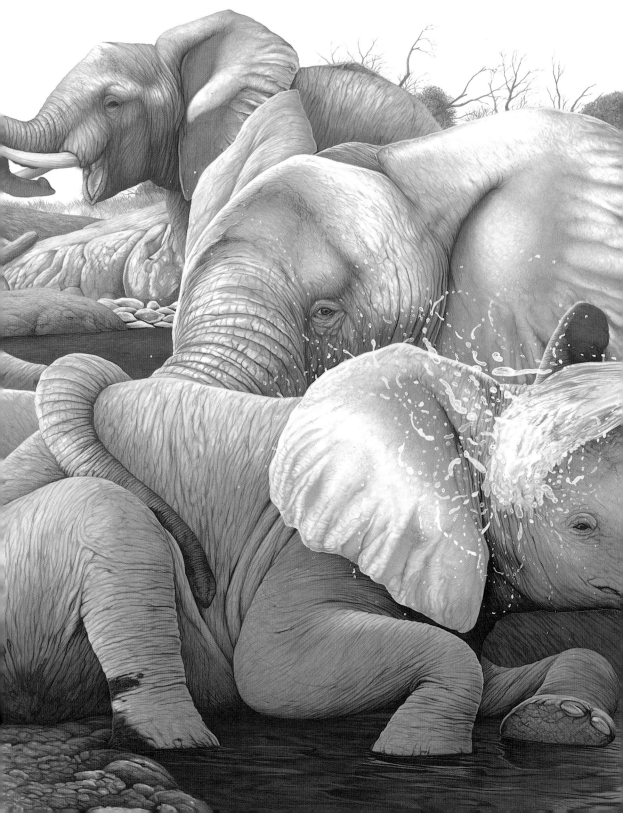

Contents

Marvelous Mammals

Mammals live all over the world in many different environments: jungles, deserts, mountains, polar regions, beneath the ground, and in the oceans. All mammals—from the tiny bumblebee bat to the gigantic blue whale—have hair, are warm-blooded, give birth to live young, and nourish them with milk.

Vertebrates vs. invertebrates
Vertebrates are animals with a backbone. They make up only 5 percent of all animal species. Mammals are vertebrates. Invertebrates are animals with no backbone. They make up 95 percent of all animal species.

Invertebrates
These include bees, butterflies, ants, and beetles.

Vertebrates
These are fish, amphibians, reptiles, birds, and mammals.

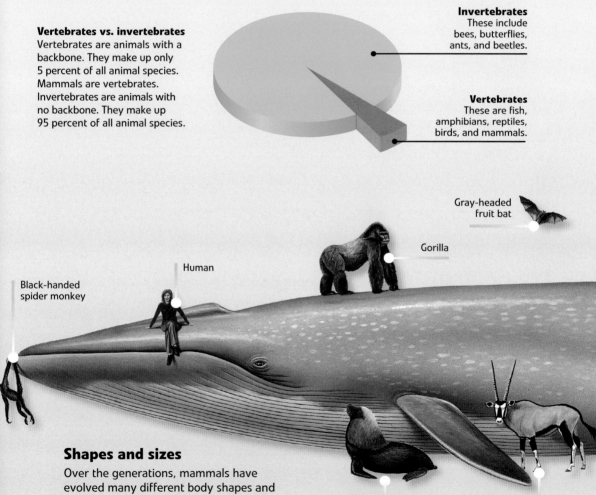

Gray-headed fruit bat

Gorilla

Human

Black-handed spider monkey

Australian sea lion

Gemsbok

Shapes and sizes
Over the generations, mammals have evolved many different body shapes and sizes, which allow them to live in vastly different environments.

MAMMAL TYPES

Mammals are divided into three different groups, depending on how their young are born. Apart from the monotremes, all mammal species give birth to live young.

Placental mammals
Most mammals, including the bush baby from Africa, are placental. Their young are nourished before birth in the mother's womb.

Monotremes
Monotremes are the only mammals to lay eggs. The Australian echidna is one of only five species of monotremes found in the world.

Marsupials
Marsupials carry and feed their young in pouches. There are more than 300 different species of marsupials, including wallabies from Australia.

That's Amazing!
The blue whale is the largest mammal on Earth. Its aorta (main blood vessel) is so large, a human could crawl through it.

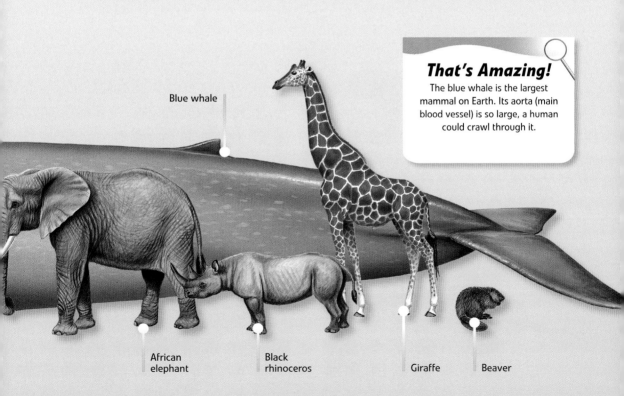

Blue whale

African elephant

Black rhinoceros

Giraffe

Beaver

Mammal Ancestors

Mammals evolved during the Triassic period, 210 million years ago—around the time that dinosaurs first appeared. The first true mammals were tiny, shrewlike animals. Earlier forms of mammals, known as therapsids, were similar in some ways to reptiles. Many of our mammal ancestors resembled animals that live on Earth today.

Dimetrodon

A meat-eating, mammal-like reptile, *Dimetrodon* lived about 280 million years ago, even before the dinosaurs.

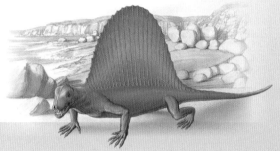

Cynognathus

Its name means "dog jaw," and *Cynognathus* looked like a dog as well. It lived about 240 million years ago.

Morganucodon

Living about 205 million years ago, *Morganucodon* was very small and looked like a mouse or a shrew.

Megazostrodon

Living about 200 million years ago, *Megazostrodon* was a small, furry nocturnal animal that ate insects and small lizards.

Uintatherium

A large, strong browsing animal with a thick skull, *Uintatherium* lived about 45 million years ago.

Arsinoitherium

These early mammals lived around 36 million years ago. They had two pairs of horns on their head.

Indricotherium

These enormous land mammals had a long neck and tusklike teeth. They lived between 26 and 40 million years ago.

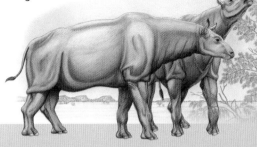

Ursavus

The small, doglike *Ursavus* was the ancestor of modern bears. It lived around 20 million years ago.

Ice-age mammals

Mammals from the last ice age (between 40,000 and 10,000 years ago) included the elephant-like woolly mammoths.

SNAP! MAMMAL LOOK-ALIKES

Some mammals look like other mammals, even though they are not related and come from completely different parts of the world.

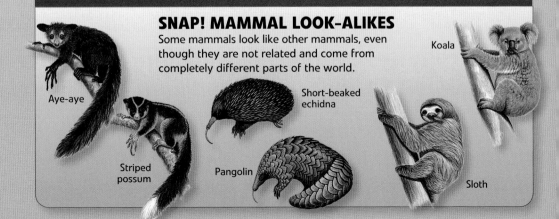

Koala

Aye-aye

Short-beaked echidna

Striped possum

Pangolin

Sloth

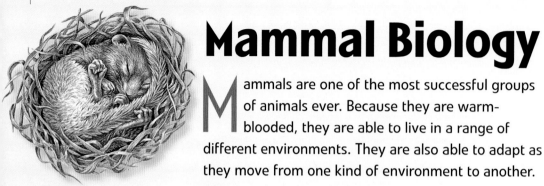

Mammal Biology

Mammals are one of the most successful groups of animals ever. Because they are warm-blooded, they are able to live in a range of different environments. They are also able to adapt as they move from one kind of environment to another.

Sleepovers

Many mammals conserve energy by sleeping through cold winters, living off the fat stored in their body. Hibernation lowers their heartbeat, breathing, and body temperature.

Making faces

After humans, wild chimpanzees are the most expressive of the primates when it comes to communicating with each other.

Playful   Aggressive   Frightened   Attentive

Hungry   Submissive

Thompson's gazelle
50 miles (81 km) per hour

Lion
50 miles (81 km) per hour

Wildebeest
50 miles (81 km) per hour

Springbok
60 miles (97 km) per hour

Pronghorn antelope
61 miles (99 km) per hour

Track star
The cheetah is the fastest land animal. It can cover up to 87 feet (26.5 m) per second at full speed.

Cheetah
68 miles (110 km) per hour

Wily wolves
Wolves work together when hunting to tire out their prey.
They communicate with each other using body language and facial
expressions, and howl to indicate their location when separated.

GIVING BIRTH

A major difference between mammals is the
way they give birth. Monotremes lay eggs.
Because placental mammals spend longer
in their mother's womb, they are more
developed at birth than marsupials.

Nourishers
The giraffe, a placental
mammal, nourishes its
baby in the womb.

Egg-layers
The platypus, a
monotreme, lays eggs
rather than giving birth to
live young.

Pouch-rearers
A baby numbat,
a marsupial, makes
its way from the
birth canal to its
mother's pouch.

Egg-layers and Pouch-rearers

Platypuses and echidnas are primitive mammals with many reptile features, including a cloaca, or chamber, for laying eggs and removing body waste. They have a lower body temperature than most mammals, and echidnas hibernate in winter. There are over 300 species of marsupials, including kangaroos, wallabies, opossums, and koalas. Most marsupials have a pouch of some kind in which they carry their young.

Echidna
The echidna has strong front limbs with thick claws for digging into hard surfaces. Its coarse fur prevents heat loss, and sharp spines protect it from predators. Echidnas burrow into soft soil to escape attack.

Male echidnas and platypuses have venomous spurs on their hind legs.

Platypus

Platypuses are perfectly adapted to live underwater. Their feet are webbed and their fur traps a layer of air next to their skin for warmth.

Koala

A newborn koala shelters in its mother's pouch, feeding on her milk. When it is more independent, it rides on her back as she feeds on leaves.

Short-beaked echidna

The sticky tongue is four times as long as its snout.

Kangaroo

There are around 60 different species of wallabies and kangaroos, most of which live in family groups. Some grow as tall as 6 feet (1.8 m).

1 Climbing in

2 Twisting around

IN THE POUCH

Kangaroo young, called joeys, push themselves into their mother's pouch headfirst. They twist and turn until they are facing the right way.

3 Ready for action

Nosing Around

More than half of all mammal species eat insects as part of their diet. Insectivores, which include small mammals such as shrews, hedgehogs, and moles, feed mainly on insects. They are often solitary, nocturnal animals that rely on smell rather than sight. Most insectivores have long, narrow snouts to sniff out their prey and sharp teeth.

Algerian
hedgehog

Giant anteater

Giant anteaters can grow to 6 feet (1.8 m) long. They live on the ground, rather than sheltering in trees as other anteaters do. Female giant anteaters carry their young on their backs.

Pyrenean
desman

A nose for every job

Algerian hedgehogs have short, pointy noses with sensitive bristles. Pyrenean desmans probe beneath underwater rocks for insects with their long, flexible snouts. European moles use their sensitive noses to smell and feel for their prey.

European
mole

FLYING MAMMALS

Bats have webbed forelimbs and are the only mammals capable of true flight. There are over 1,200 different species, from the tiny Kitti's hog-nosed bat to the giant golden-winged flying fox.

Hanging around
Gray-headed flying foxes hunt at night. During the day they group together in trees, hanging upside down.

Echolocation
Bats send out a series of ultrasonic sounds to detect and catch their prey.

Sounds bounce off the bat's prey and echo back, revealing its location.

A bat sends out rapid clicking sounds.

As the bat gets closer to its prey, the frequency of clicks increases.

The bat captures its prey.

That's Amazing!
Giant anteaters do not have any teeth. They use their long tongues to lap up the thousands of ants and termites they swallow whole every day.

Primates

Primates are divided into two groups. The higher group contains monkeys, apes, and humans. They have large brains, good eyesight, and a highly developed sense of touch. Lemurs, bush babies, lorises, and tarsiers make up the lower group. They still have much in common with their insect-eating ancestors. Most primates live in tropical regions, where food is easy to find.

Gorilla hand   Gorilla foot

HANDS AND FEET

Gorillas gather leaves, bark, and fruits with their flexible hands. Indris use their hands and feet to climb trees. Aye-ayes hook insect larvae from tree holes with their long, slender fingers.

Indri hand   Indri foot

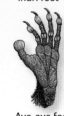

Aye-aye hand   Aye-aye foot

Eyes and ears
Tarsiers live in the rain forests of Southeast Asia. They leap from branch to branch, hunting for food. They have large ears and eyes, with eyeballs the same size as their brain.

Chimpanzees can be taught to communicate with humans using special symbols for different actions and objects.

Gentle giants

Gorillas might look fierce, but they are actually gentle vegetarians. Each night, they build a warm nest in the treetops, safe from predators. Gorillas live in family groups, moving through the mountain forests of eastern and central Africa to find food. Each family is headed by a large silverback male, which drives other males away by roaring and beating his chest.

Lionesses hunt together. They sneak up on their prey then make a quick rush at it for the kill.

Silent and deadly

There are over 35 different types of cats, ranging from the tiny South American oncilla to the majestic Siberian tiger. All cats hunt in similar ways, silently stalking their prey until it is time to attack. They rush at it, wrestling it to the ground and holding it down with their claws, then finish it off by biting its neck or throat.

Carnivores

Carnivore means "meat eater." Carnivorous mammals have long canine teeth so that they can grip and kill prey easily. Their incisors strip flesh from bones, and their carnassial teeth slice through their food, rather than grinding it as the flat molar teeth of herbivores do. Not all carnivores eat only meat—many eat plants as well. Although some carnivores are social animals, most are solitary, preferring to hunt alone.

Hyena

Raccoon

Ocelot

THE CARNIVORES

Carnivores are found all over the
world. There are seven families of
carnivores: dogs, cats, bears (including
the giant panda), raccoons, civets,
hyenas, and a group made up of
weasels, martens, otters, skunks,
and badgers.

Weasel

Dog

Civet

Grizzly
bear

Grazers and Browsers

Mammals find food in many different ways. Grazers, such as the white rhinoceros, feed mainly on grasses. The white rhinoceros has a broad upper lip that helps it pluck short, stubbly grass. The black rhinoceros, however, is a browser. It has a pointed upper lip to help it pluck fleshy leaves, buds, and flowers from trees.

Rhinoceroses
All five species of rhinoceroses are herbivores, eating either leaves or grass. They feed mainly at night, and can survive for several days without water.

Gerenuks
East African gerenuks, or giraffe-gazelles, are so well adapted to desert life they never need to drink. They collect moisture from the tender leaves of prickly bushes and trees.

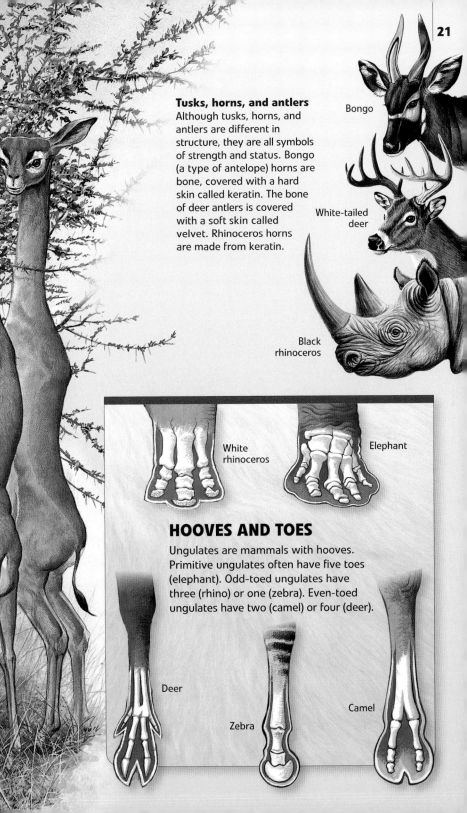

Tusks, horns, and antlers

Although tusks, horns, and antlers are different in structure, they are all symbols of strength and status. Bongo (a type of antelope) horns are bone, covered with a hard skin called keratin. The bone of deer antlers is covered with a soft skin called velvet. Rhinoceros horns are made from keratin.

Bongo

White-tailed deer

Black rhinoceros

White rhinoceros

Elephant

HOOVES AND TOES

Ungulates are mammals with hooves. Primitive ungulates often have five toes (elephant). Odd-toed ungulates have three (rhino) or one (zebra). Even-toed ungulates have two (camel) or four (deer).

Deer

Zebra

Camel

Chewers and Burrowers

Rodents can be found all over the world, from the desert to the Arctic. They range in size from the matchbox-sized pygmy jerboa to the capybara, which can weigh up to 110 pounds (50 kg). Some species, such as squirrels, live in trees, while others, such as prairie dogs, share group burrows. Beavers spend most of their time in water. Insectivores, such as moles, spend almost their entire lives underground.

Dam builders
Both European and North American beavers eat bark and leaves, and live in water. They build large nests, called lodges, and protect them from predators by damming streams to form ponds too big to cross.

Tunnel world
Moles trap and store earthworms and grubs in a complex network of underground tunnels. The tunnels are also used for sleeping and for rearing their young.

Shaft linking tunnel system to surface

Tunnel network

Mole tunnels can be as long as 660 feet (200 m).

Food store
Moles remove the heads from earthworms then pull them through their claws to remove any grit. They store live worms in a chamber to eat later.

Mole seizing prey in foraging tunnel

Nesting burrow for young

RODENT ROUNDUP

More than a third of mammal species are rodents. South American capybaras, the largest rodents, are excellent swimmers. Although lemmings live in Arctic regions, they do not hibernate. Black rats are agile climbers. The crested porcupine defends itself by rattling its quills.

Black rat

Capybara

Crested porcupine

Lemming

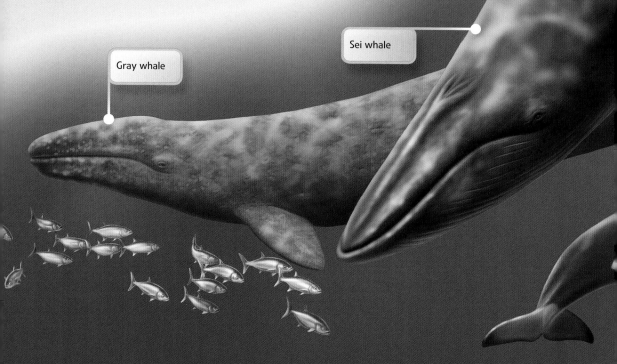

Dwindling dugongs
Although dugongs could once be found in large numbers in the Indian Ocean, only a small number is now left, mainly in the waters of northern Australia. Sea-grass beds provide food and shelter.

Ocean Dwellers

There are three different groups of mammals that live in the water: cetaceans (whales, dolphins, and porpoises), sirenians (dugongs and manatees), and pinnipeds (walruses, sea lions, and seals). Pinnipeds also spend time on land. Sea lions can turn their hind flippers around to walk on, while true seals move like caterpillars when out of the water. Although they resemble fish, whales are warm-blooded, and give birth to live young, which they suckle on milk.

Sei whale

Gray whale

Fact or Fiction?

Whale sharks look like whales and feed on similar food. But they are fish rather than mammals, and use gills to breathe underwater.

Surface breathers

Whales spend most of their time underwater. However, unlike fish, they need to come to the surface to breathe. They take in air through blowholes on top of their head.

SEA LIONS

Sea lions are extremely well adapted to life at sea. They can swim a month after birth, and slow their heartbeat from 100 beats per minute to 10 beats per minute when diving. They often hunt for squid or fish as a team.

Killer whale

Australian sea lions

Fun Facts

Tusk power
A male walrus's tusks can grow as long as 2 feet 3 inches (68 cm).

Mammals are amazing. They can produce their own body heat from the food they eat, and their young can learn from experience, making them the most successful of all animal groups. Find out more astonishing mammal facts.

SHOUT IT OUT

Male howler monkeys are the loudest land animals. Their voices can be heard clearly 3 miles (4.8 km) away. Howler monkeys are native to the tropical forests of South and Central America.

MOST UNLIKELY RELATIVES

The hyrax weighs up to 11 pounds (5 kg) and its closest relative, the elephant, can weigh up to 15,400 pounds (7,000 kg).

Elephant

Hyrax

True mates
Gibbons are one of the few primates that mate for life.

Racing heartbeat
The tiny shrew's heart beats 1,000 times per minute. A human heart beats 60 times per minute.

STRIPY HORSE

What do you get when you cross a zebra with a horse? A zorse, of course! Because it is a hybrid—a mix of two species—the zorse cannot reproduce.

COBRA VS. MONGOOSE

The mongoose is immune to snake venom, so it can eat poisonous snakes, such as cobras. The mongoose moves quickly around the cobra, then kills it by biting its neck.

Sun lovers
Ring-tailed lemurs love sunbathing, stretching out their bodies to catch maximum rays.

Blood lappers
Blood-drinking vampire bats have razor-sharp front teeth. They hunt only when it is completely dark.

BRAINIACS

A sperm whale has the largest brain of any animal—more than five times heavier than a human's.

Peanut in a pouch
Baby wallabies are only the size of a peanut when they are born.

JUMBO-SIZED

An elephant's trunk is sensitive enough to pull up a blade of grass, and strong enough to uproot a whole tree. An elephant also uses its trunk to spray itself with water or mud.

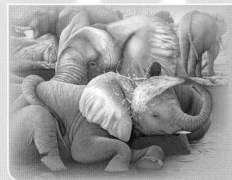

Clown face
Mandrills have the most colorful faces of all the monkeys, with bright red noses and blue cheeks.

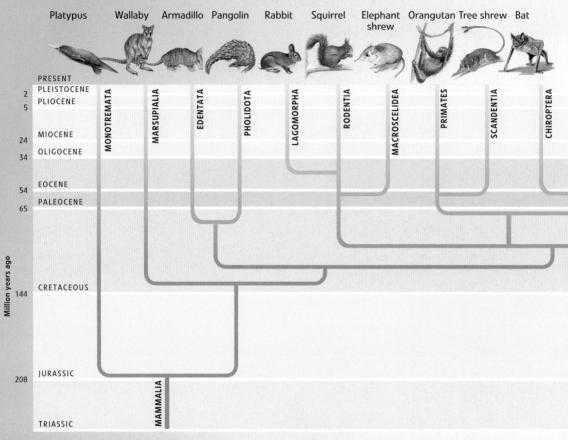

Million years ago

Platypus	Wallaby	Armadillo	Pangolin	Rabbit	Squirrel	Elephant shrew	Orangutan	Tree shrew	Bat

PRESENT
PLEISTOCENE
2
PLIOCENE
5

MIOCENE
24
OLIGOCENE
34

EOCENE
54
PALEOCENE
65

CRETACEOUS
144

JURASSIC
208

TRIASSIC

MONOTREMATA · MARSUPIALIA · EDENTATA · PHOLIDOTA · LAGOMORPHA · RODENTIA · MACROSCELIDEA · PRIMATES · SCANDENTIA · CHIROPTERA

MAMMALIA

Classifying Mammals

While mammals include monotremes and marsupials, most species belong to the placental group. The three largest orders are Rodentia (including mice and rats), Chiroptera (bats), and Soricomorpha (shrews and moles). Primates (including humans) are the sixth-largest group.

ORDERS OF MAMMALS

Mammals (class Mammalia) are a group of around 5,400 species of vertebrates. The class can be further broken down into the various orders of mammals, which include:

Monotremata The species are the platypus, and 4 species of echidnas.

Marsupialia There are more than 300 species of these pouched mammals, including koalas and kangaroos.

Edentata The 29 species of anteaters, sloths, and armadillos live in Central and South America.

Pholidota The 8 species of pangolins (scaly anteaters) live in Africa and Southeast Asia.

Lagomorpha About 80 species of rabbits, pikas, and hares are native to Africa, Europe, Asia, and North and South America.

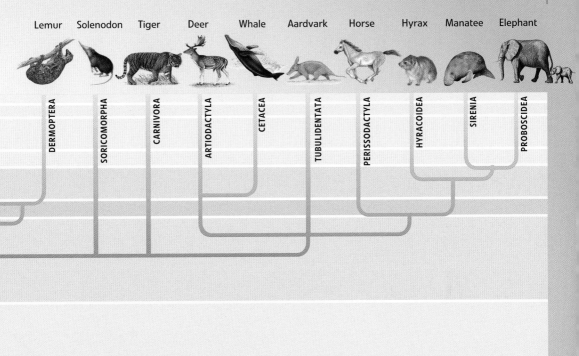

Lemur | Solenodon | Tiger | Deer | Whale | Aardvark | Horse | Hyrax | Manatee | Elephant

DERMOPTERA | SORICOMORPHA | CARNIVORA | ARTIODACTYLA | CETACEA | TUBULIDENTATA | PERISSODACTYLA | HYRACOIDEA | SIRENIA | PROBOSCIDEA

Rodentia This is the largest mammal order, with more than 2,000 species. They are found everywhere except Antarctica.

Macroscelidea The 17 species of insect-eating elephant shrews are found only in Africa.

Primates Most of the 300–400 species are monkeys, tarsiers, and tree-dwelling prosimians, such as lemurs. The apes are the largest of the primates.

Scandentia The 20 species of tree shrews live in Asia. Only one species is nocturnal.

Chiroptera There are more than 1,200 species of bats, the second-largest order of mammals.

Dermoptera The 2 species of colugos (flying lemurs) live in Southeast Asia.

Soricomorpha There are more than 300 species, which include tiny shrews, moles, and solenodons.

Carnivora There are more than 280 species of meat-eating animals, and they are found on almost every continent.

Artiodactyla There are around 220 species of even-toed hoofed mammals. These include camels, giraffes, hippopotamuses, and goats.

Cetacea About 90 species of whales, dolphins, and porpoises are found in all the world's seas.

Tubulidentata The short-legged, long-nosed aardvark is the only species in this order, and it lives in the Sahara.

Perissodactyla The 17 species of horses, tapirs, and rhinoceroses are native to Africa, Asia, and South America.

Hyracoidea The 4 species of rabbit-like hyraxes live in Africa and the Middle East.

Sirenia There are 4 species of manatees and dugongs.

Proboscidea The elephant is the largest land mammal. There are 2 species: African and Asian.

Over To You

Research the following records to create a Mammal Hall of Fame. Some of the information can be found in this book.

1 Largest mammal

2 Smallest mammal

3 Tallest mammal

4 Fastest mammal

5 Slowest mammal

6 Loudest mammal

7 Loudest mammal on land

8 Smelliest mammal

9 Mammal with the thickest skin

10 Mammal with the longest life span

Answers: 1 blue whale **2** bumblebee bat (also known as Kitti's hog-nosed bat) **3** giraffe **4** cheetah **5** sloth **6** blue whale **7** howler monkey **8** striped skunk **9** rhinoceros **10** bowhead whale

Glossary

ancestor (AN-ses-ter)
An early type of animal from which a later type evolves.

carnassial teeth
(kar-NA-sea-ul TEETH) Cheek teeth with sharp, scissor-like edges used by carnivores to tear up food.

carnivore
(KAHR-neh-vor) An animal that eats mainly meat.

environment
(en-VY-ern-ment)
The physical surroundings of an animal that affect its development and behavior.

herbivore
(ER-buh-vor) An animal that eats only plant material, such as roots, leaves, and seeds.

hibernate (HY-bur-nayt)
To sleep during the winter months, living off stored fat and conserving energy by slowing down heartbeat and breathing until spring.

incisors (in-SY-zurz) The front teeth of an animal, used for cutting food.

insectivore
(in-SEK-tih-vor) An animal that eats only or mainly insects or invertebrates.

invertebrate
(in-VER-teh-bret) An animal without a backbone.

mammal (MA-mul)
A warm-blooded vertebrate that suckles its young with milk and has a single bone in its lower jaw. Most mammals have hair or fur and give birth to live young.

marsupial
(mahr-SOO-pee-ul) A mammal that gives birth to young which are not fully developed. The young are suckled in a pouch until ready to move around independently.

monotreme
(MA-nuh-tream) A primitive egg-laying mammal with many features in common with reptiles.

nocturnal (nok-TUR-nul)
Describes an animal that moves around at night and rests during daylight hours.

placental mammal
(pluh-SEN-til MA-mul)
A mammal that nourishes its developing young inside its body with a blood-rich organ called a placenta.

predator (PREH-duh-ter)
An animal that lives by hunting and eating other animals.

primate
(PRY-mayt)
A member of the highest order of animals, with flexible hands and feet, good eyesight, and a highly developed brain.

rodent
(ROH-dent)
A small placental mammal with large front teeth used for gnawing or nibbling.

ungulate
(UNG-gyuh-lut)
A large, plant-eating mammal with hooves.

vertebrate
(VER-tih-brit)
An animal with a backbone.

Index

Websites

Due to the changing nature of Internet links, PowerKids Press has developed an online list of websites related to the subject of this book. This site is updated regularly. Please use this link to access the list:

www.powerkidslinks.com/disc/fam/